TANGRAM PUZZLES

PUZZLES

500 TRICKY SHAPES TO CONFOUND & ASTOUND

Chris Crawford

Sterling Publishing Co., Inc.

New York

CONTENTS

10 9 8 7 6 5

Published by Sterling Publishing Co., Inc.
387 Park Avenue South, New York, N.Y. 10016
© 2002 by Chris Crawford
Distributed in Canada by Sterling Publishing
C/o Canadian Manda Group, One Atlantic Avenue, Suite 105
Toronto, Ontario, Canada M6K 3E7
Distributed in Great Britain and Europe by Chris Lloyd at Orca Book
Services, Stanley House, Fleets Lane, Poole BH15 3AJ, England.
Distributed in Australia by Capricorn Link (Australia) Pty. Ltd.
P.O. Box 704, Windsor, NSW 2756 Australia

Printed in China
All rights reserved

Sterling ISBN 0-8069-7589-X

Who would guess that myriad forms and figures are hiding in an unassuming square? Welcome to the wonderful world of tangrams. The tangram set is a square that has been divided into seven simple shapes, which are called *tans*. These include two large triangles, two smaller triangles, a medium triangle, a square, and a parallelogram. The shapes aren't much more exciting than the square they started as, but when manipulated properly, these most basic shapes can convey the ideas, thoughts, and emotions of the player. Or they can be just plain fun.

HISTORY

Tangrams is an ancient Chinese game. No one is quite sure when they first came about or who invented them. Some think it was Chinese mathematicians over 1,000 years ago. Ronald Read, of the University of Waterloo, theorizes that tangrams are only about 200 years old. Tangrams were mentioned in a book in 1854, which was a reprint of a book from the 1700s. The name is also a mystery. A very believable theory is that it comes from *tramgram*, an obsolete English word meaning "puzzle" or "trinket." Another, less likely, theory is that a tile maker named Tan accidentally invented them when he dropped a tile and it broke into the seven shapes we know of today.

Tangrams became very popular in the United States, Asia, and Europe in the 1800s. It's likely that the game was introduced to the Western world by sailors and traders who brought sets back after visiting the port of Canton in China. Canton was the only Chinese port where whites could trade at the time. The game was played by young and old, male and female, rich and poor. Many famous people were known to enjoy the game, including Lewis Carroll, Edgar Allan Poe, Napoleon, and John Quincy Adams.

In 1903, Sam Loyd wrote a book called *The Eighth Book of Tan*. It told the story of the god Tan, who invented tangrams 4,000 years ago. Tan wrote seven books, each containing 1,000 figures, that showed the progress of the human race. The designs

began with the creation of man and continued far beyond what we understand. Loyd backed his story up with references to supposed scholars who had, in fact, seen the first and second books of Tan. He also claimed to have remnants of one of the books in his possession. While it was a fascinating story and had many wonderful tangrams to solve, it was later found to be a hoax. Unfortunately, many people took it quite seriously, and Loyd's story led to a misunderstanding that remains to this day.

HOW TO PLAY

Playing tangrams can be as simple or as difficult as you want to make it. Sometimes the shapes form easily. Other times, they can be quite frustrating. Tangrams have the habit of being deceptive in their simplicity. When you start to look at the large variety of figures, the paradox, and the snug shapes (to be explained shortly), the challenges become more apparent. The way *you* decide to play tangrams is limited only by your imagination.

CLASSIC

This is for one player and is the most common way to play. All that is needed is a standard set of tangram pieces, or *tans*, and a flat surface. The idea is to manipulate the pieces to create a shape. All pieces must touch, lying flat with no overlapping. Usually, the shape to be made is in the form of a silhouette, like the ones in this book, but you might want to try making a new shape depicting an interesting object. Making two separate definable shapes from a single set is another challenging variation.

CLASSIC DOUBLE

This is played the same way as classic, but uses two sets of *tans*. It makes larger and more intricate shapes possible, but also sometimes adds to the difficulty of the puzzle. A greater number of pieces is quite helpful when creating new shapes, but it can be hard to use them all.

PLAYER VS. PLAYER

This is a game for two or more players. One set of *tans* is needed per player. A silhouette is chosen, and the players compete to see who can make it first. Another way to play is to have each player choose a shape for the other to solve. You may also try making the most figures in a given amount of time.

STORIES

The many shapes available lend themselves to storytelling. They have been used to illustrate a number of children's books. Check your local library for these or any other interesting tales. Try to pick out figures to go with some of your favorites, or even make up your own story.

TYPES

STANDARD

Standard puzzles are any shapes that use all seven *tans*. All pieces must touch each other in at least one spot. Most tangram puzzles fall into this category. There are also some designs related to this type that have all the pieces used but not touching.

PARADOX

Paradox puzzles are one of the most interesting ways tangrams can be put together. Using all seven *tans*, almost identical designs can be made, but one silhouette appears to have an extra or missing piece. A good example of a paradox puzzle is the pair of humanoid figures, one of which appears to be the same as the other, only missing a foot. Sam Loyd created this example, along with many other wonderful paradox puzzles.

CONVEX

A convex tangram is a shape where all corners stick out and there are no indentations. A line drawn from any point to another will stay inside the figure. In an article published in

American Mathematical Monthly, Fu Tsiang Wan and Chuan-Chin Hsing proved that there are only 13 possible convex shapes that can be made with a standard set of *tans*.

SNUG

This is a set whose true size is unknown. Ronald Read theorized that a snug tangram is one in which the small *tans* are in contact with the large ones along their entire edge. There are no over-hangs or places where a small *tan* is touching only one point to the side of another *tan*.

Tangrams have entertained people for ages and will continue to do so. Fun for even the youngest, they offer many challenges to anyone interested in puzzles. One of the best things about them is that you're not limited to what you have to make or solve. It's up to you! Enjoy.

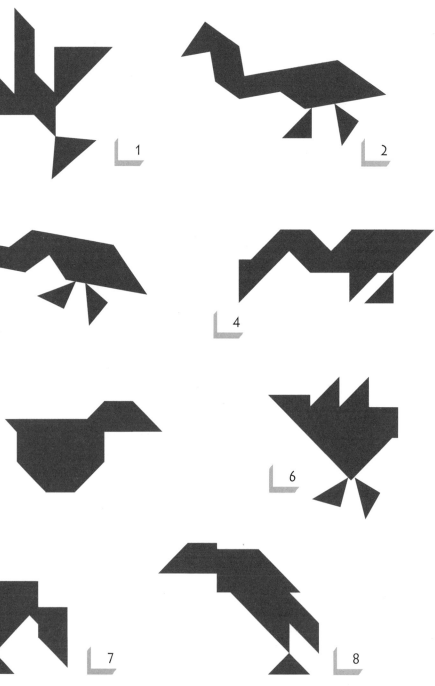

9

10

11

12

13

14

15

16

17

18

19

20

21

22

23

24

25

26

27

28

29

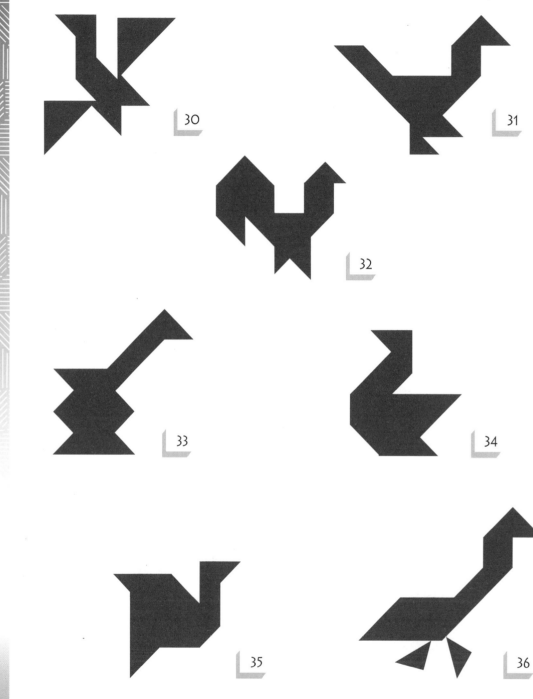

30

31

32

33

34

35

36

37

38

39

40

41

42

43

1

2

3

4

5

6

7

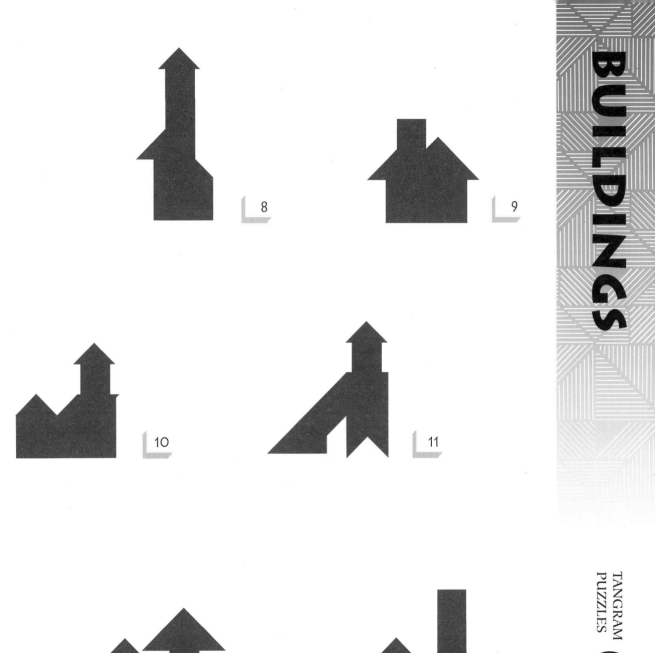

8

9

10

11

12

13

14

15

16

17

18

19

1

2

3

4

5

6

7

8

9

10

11

12

13

14

15

16

17

1

2

3

4

5

6

7

8

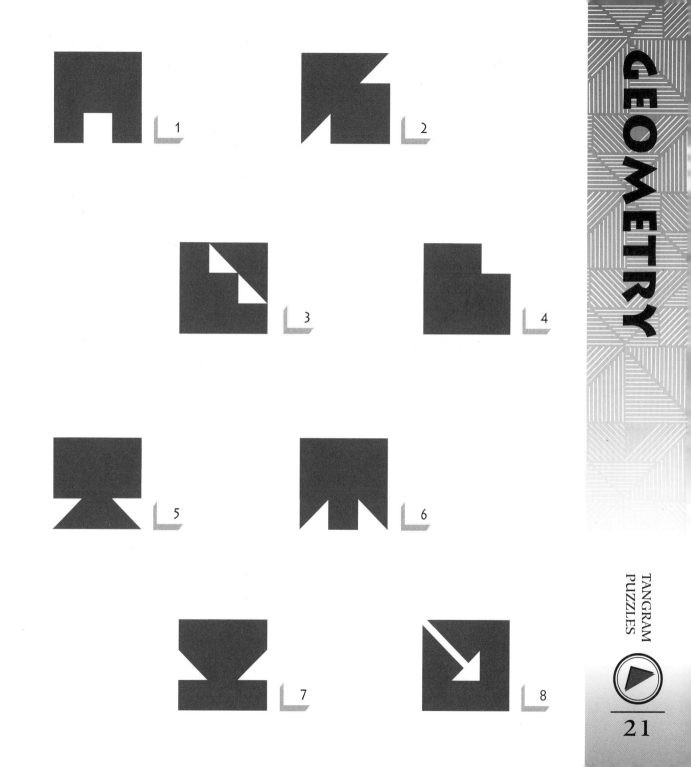

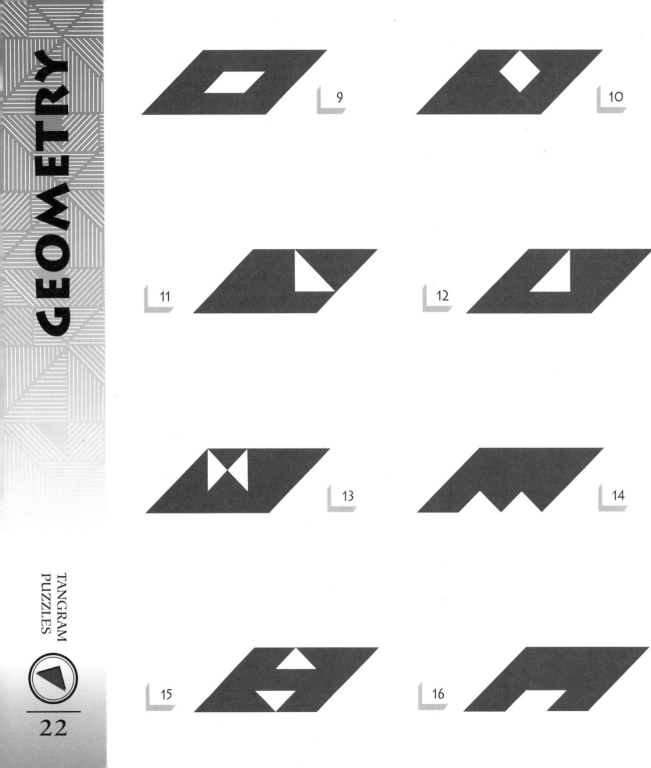

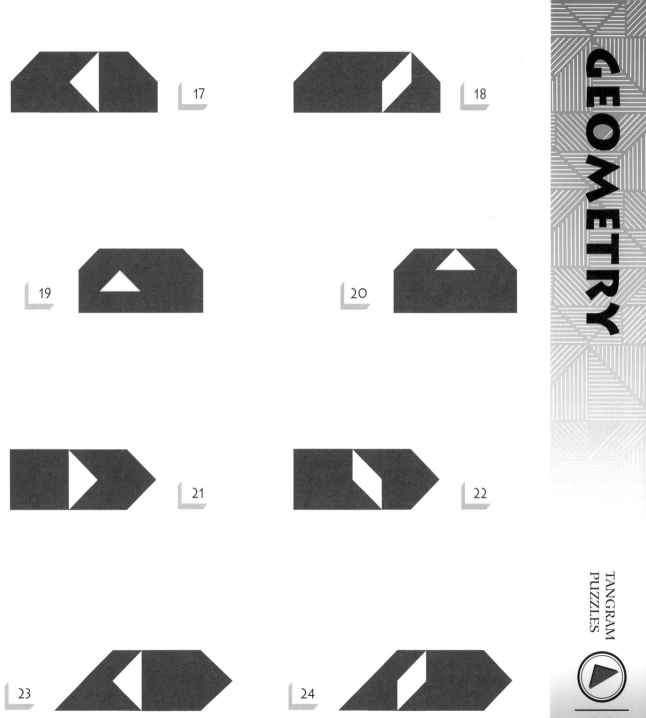

17

18

19

20

21

22

23

24

1

2

3

4

5

6

7

8

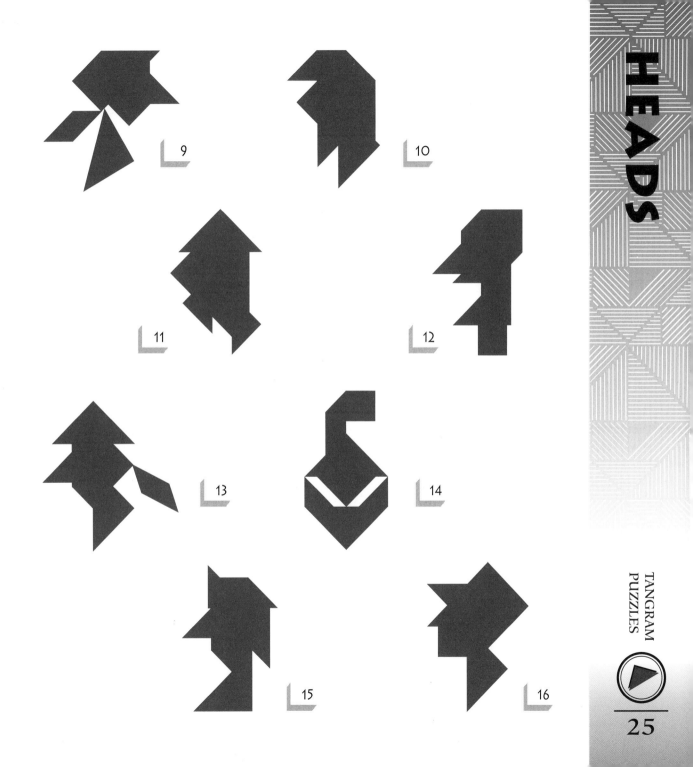

9

10

11

12

13

14

15

16

17

18

19

20

21

22

23

24

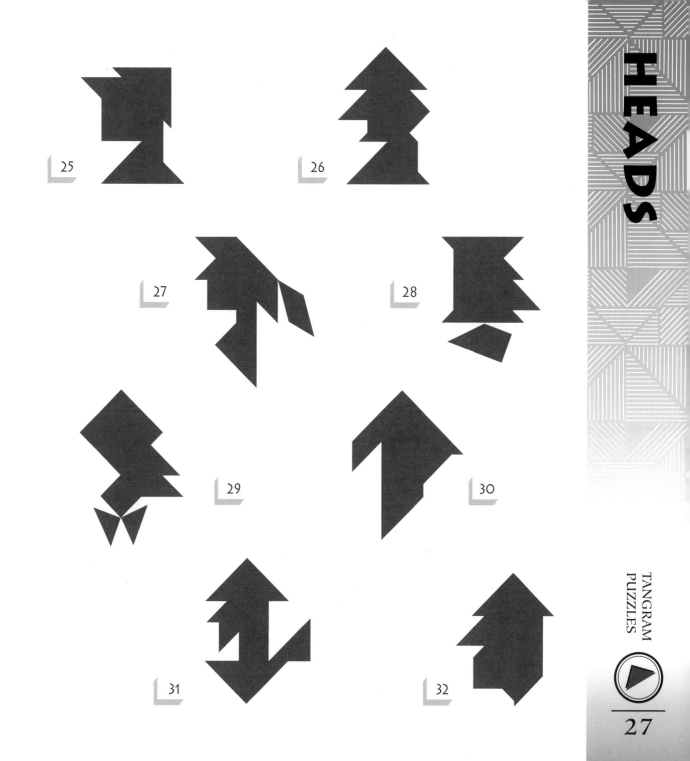

25

26

27

28

29

30

31

32

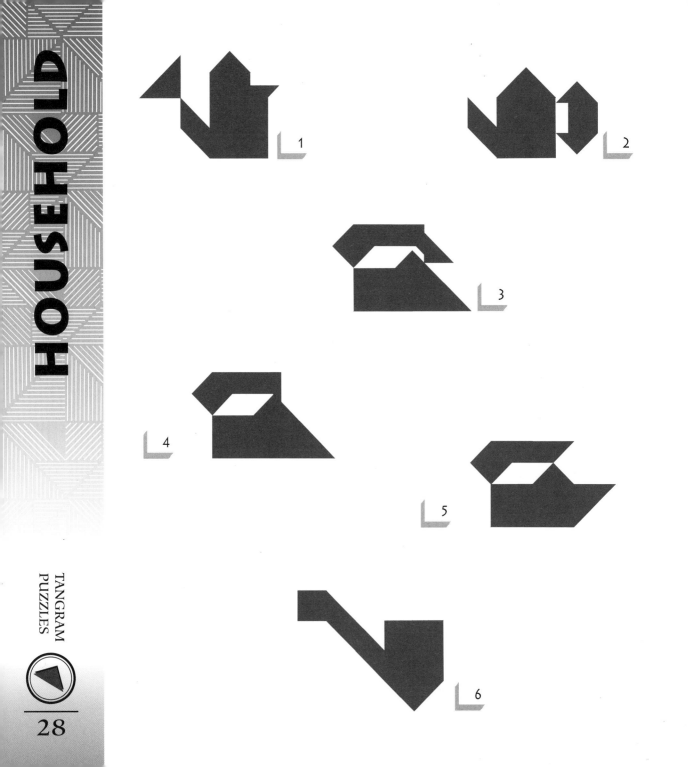

1

2

3

4

5

6

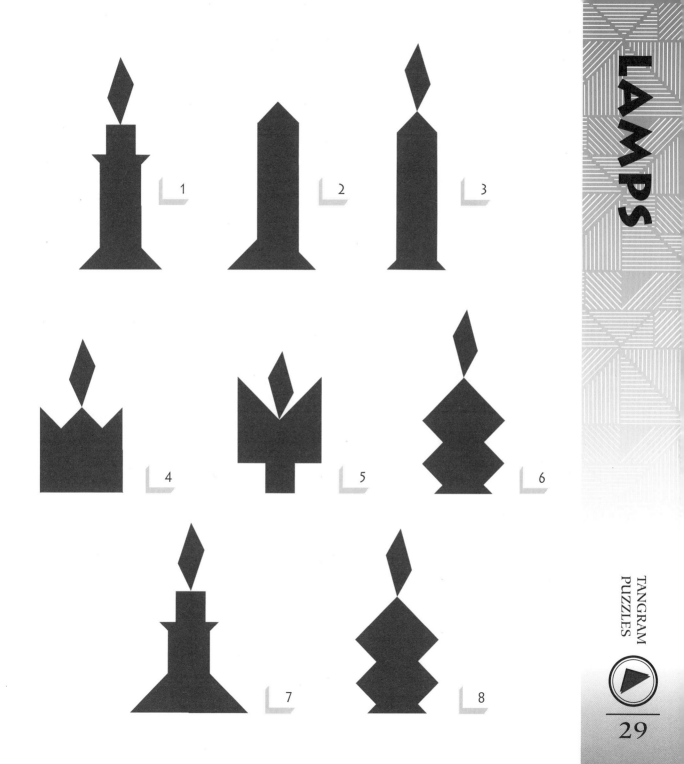

9

10

11

12

13

14

15

16

17

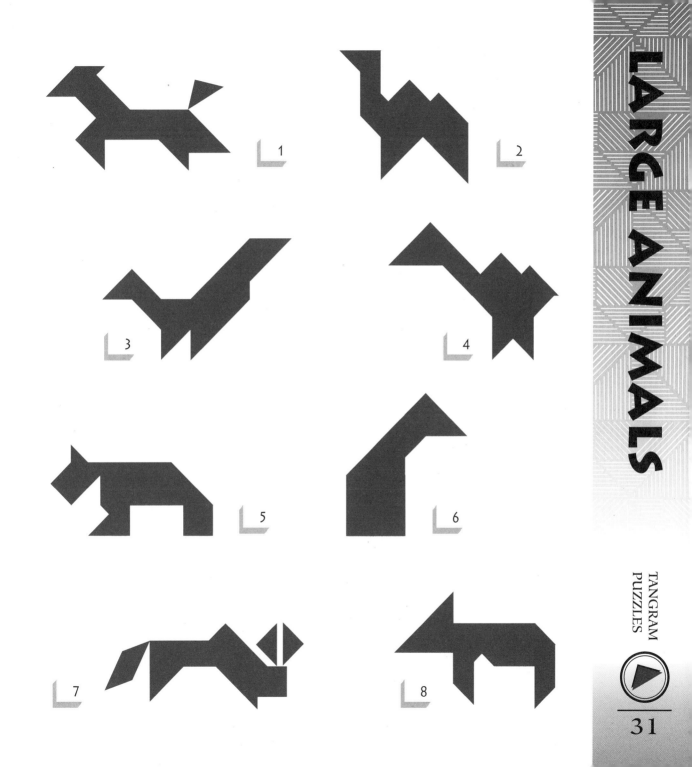

1

2

3

4

5

6

7

8

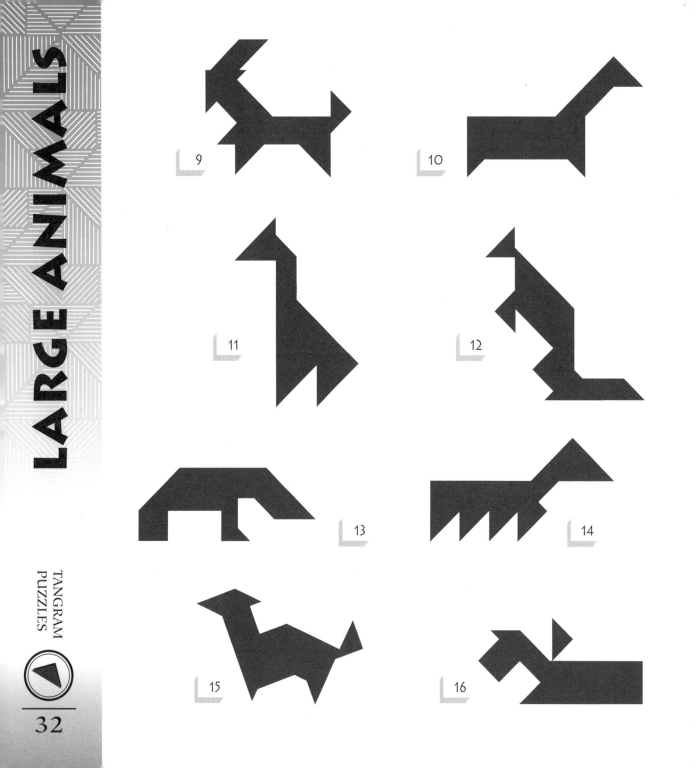

9

10

11

12

13

14

15

16

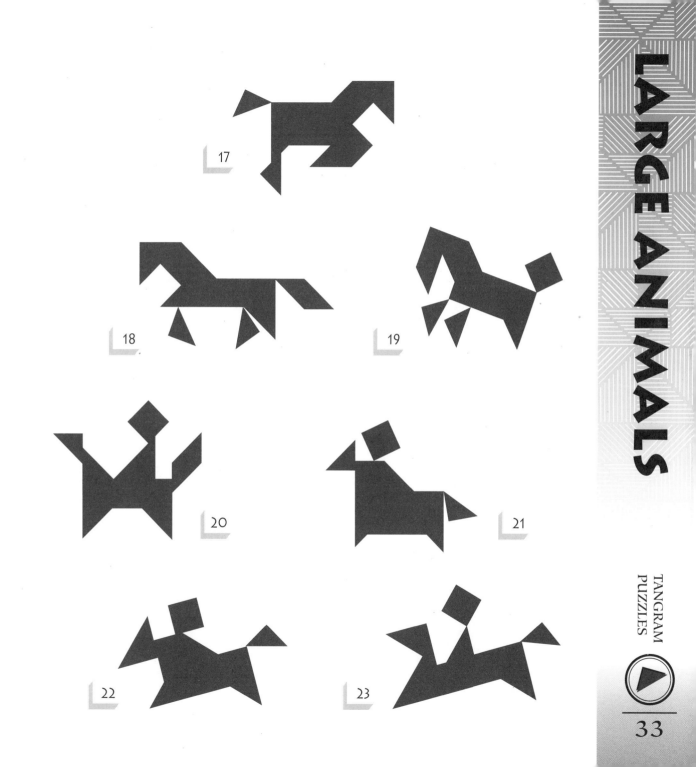

17

18

19

20

21

22

23

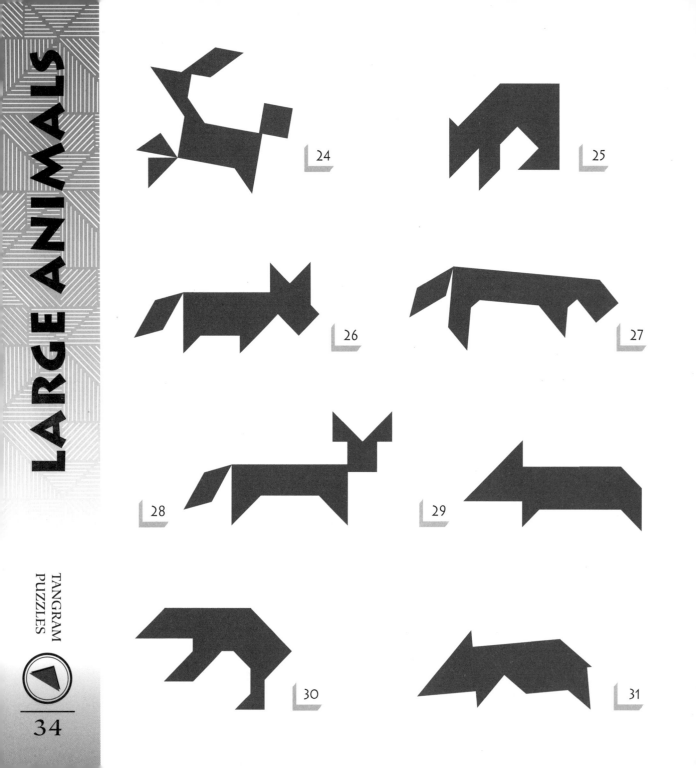

24

25

26

27

28

29

30

31

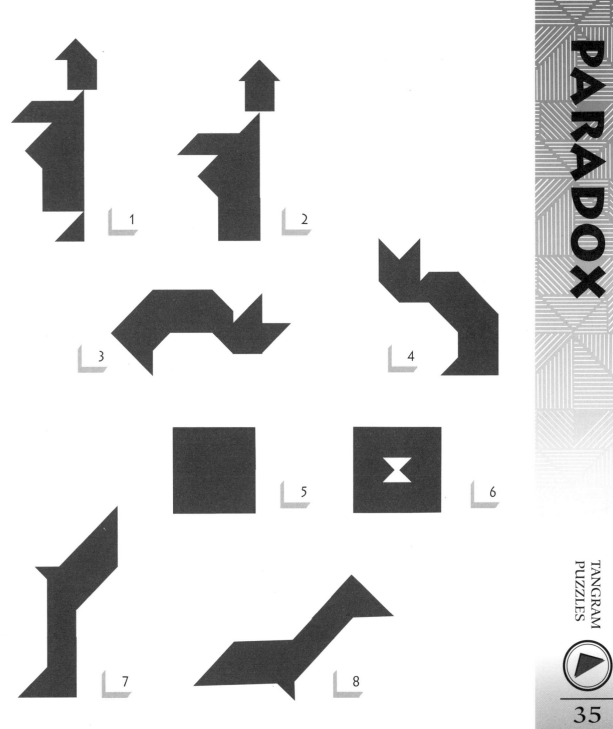

9

10

11

12

13

14

15

1

2

3

4

5

6

7

15

16

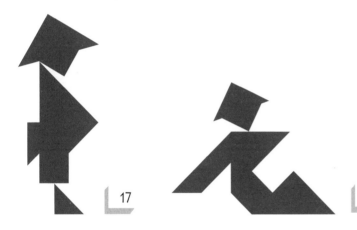

17

18

19

20

21

22

23

24

25

26

27

28

29

30

31

32

33

34

35

36

37

38

39

40

41

42

43

44

45

46

47

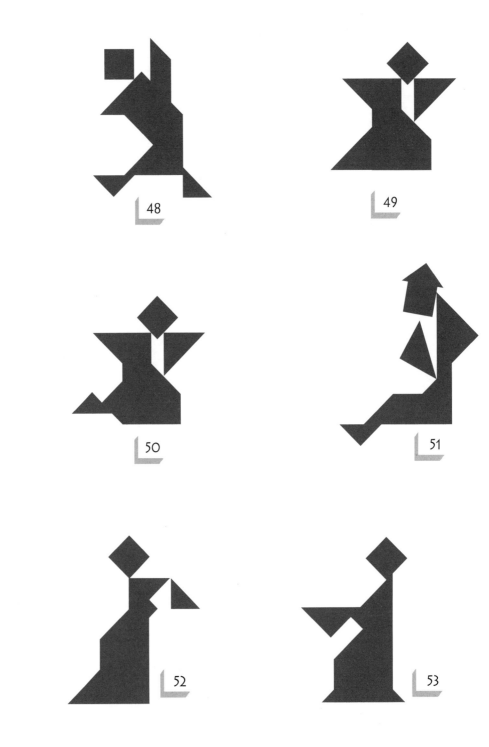

48

49

50

51

52

53

1

2

3

4

5

6

7

7

8

9

10

11

12

13

14

15

16

17

18

19

20

21

22

23

24

25

26

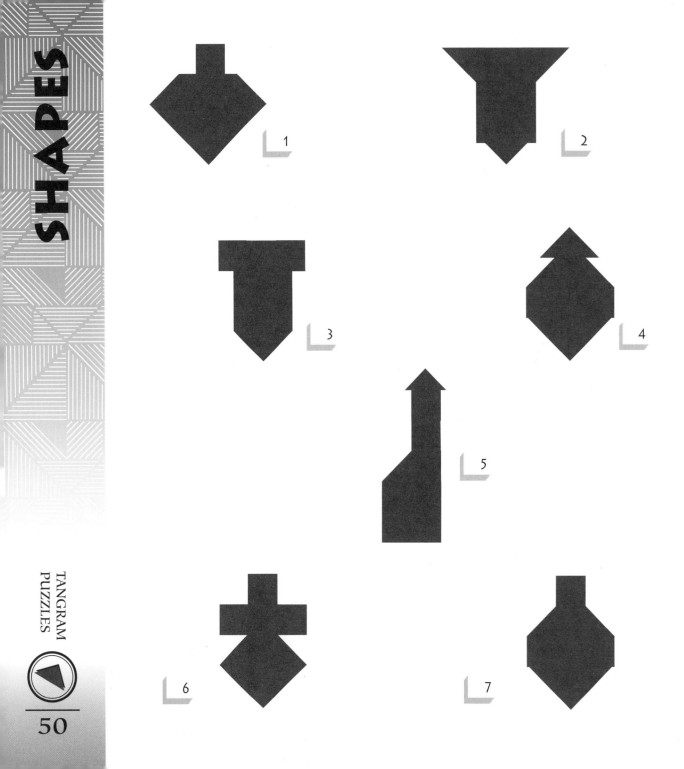

1

2

3

4

5

6

7

8

9

10

11

12

13

14

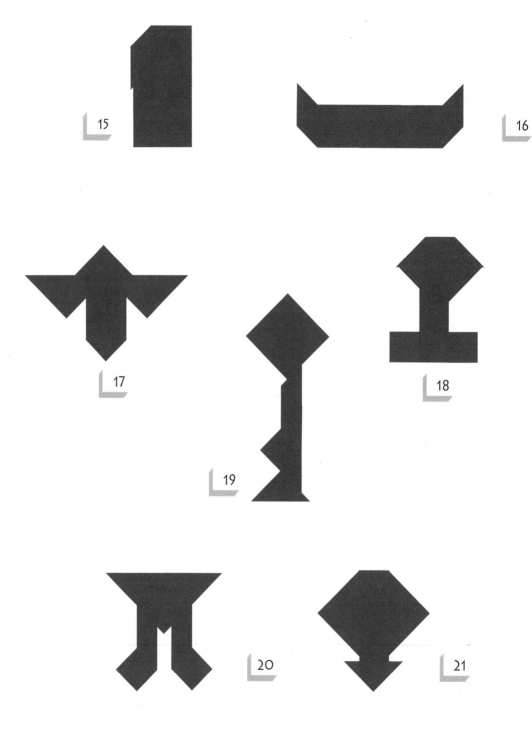

15

16

17

18

19

20

21

22

23

24

25

26

27

28

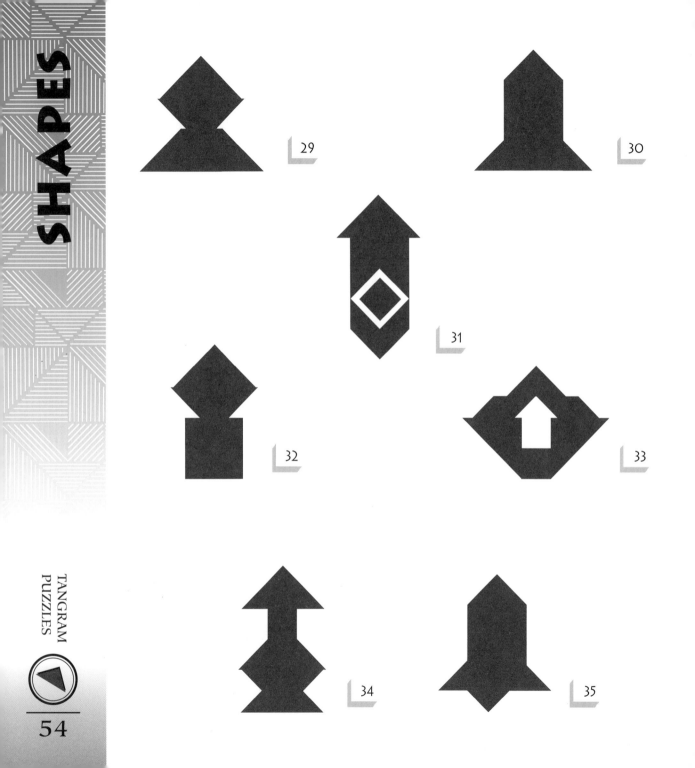

29

30

31

32

33

34

35

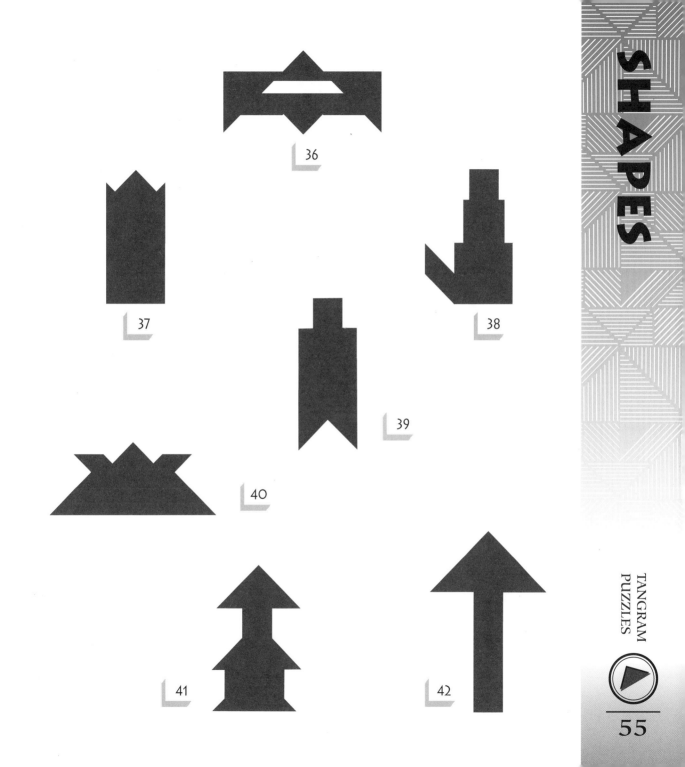

36

37

38

39

40

41

42

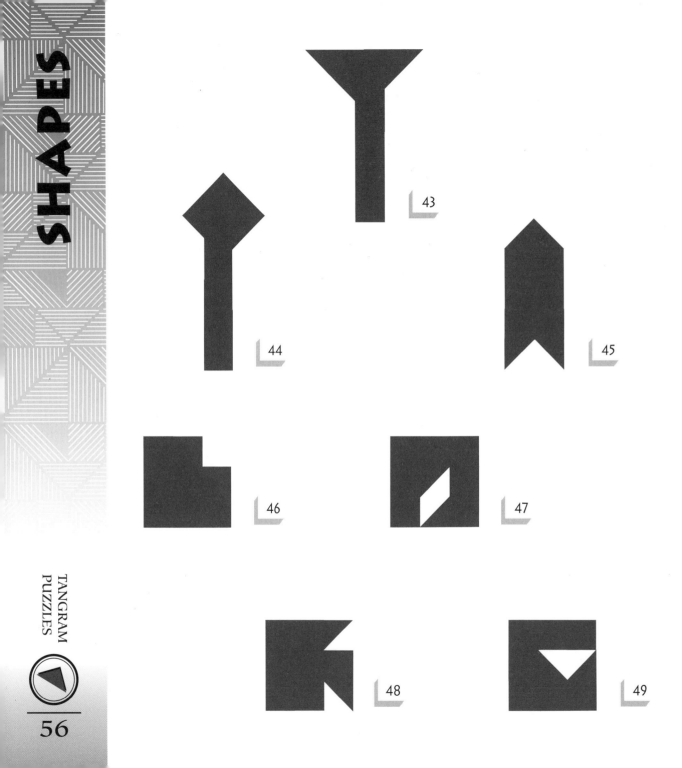

43

44

45

46

47

48

49

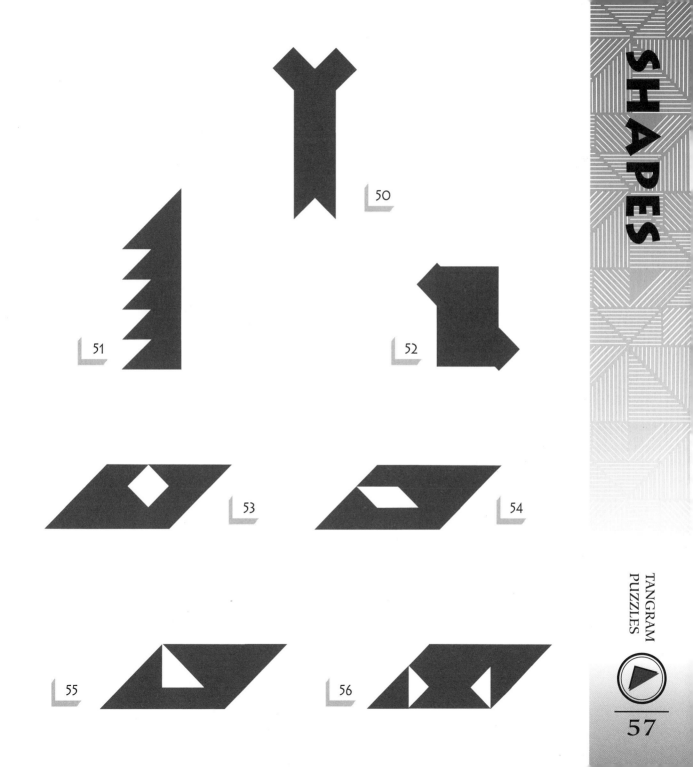

50

51

52

53

54

55

56

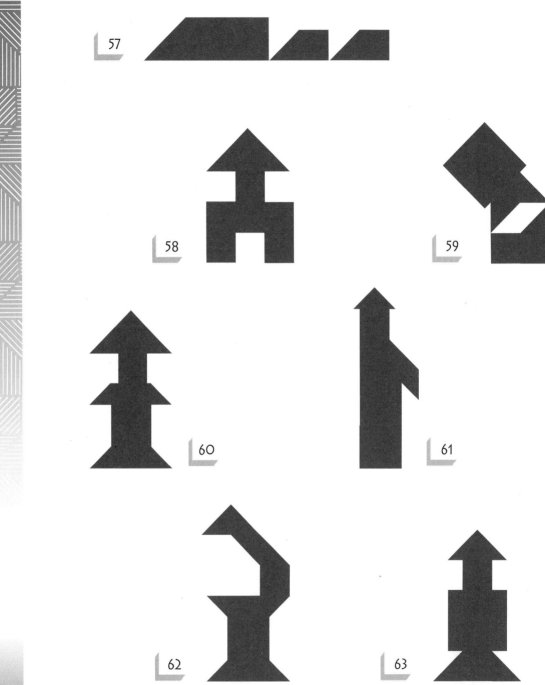

57

58

59

60

61

62

63

64

65

66

67

68

69

70

1

2

3

4

5

6

7

1

2

3

4

5

6

7

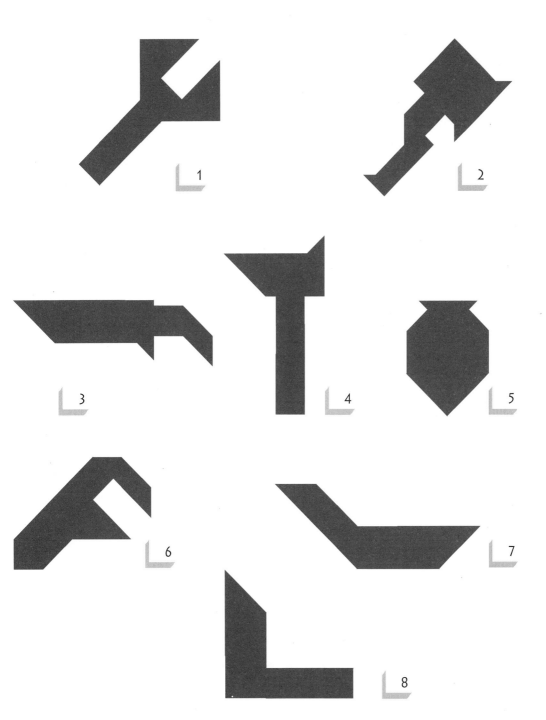

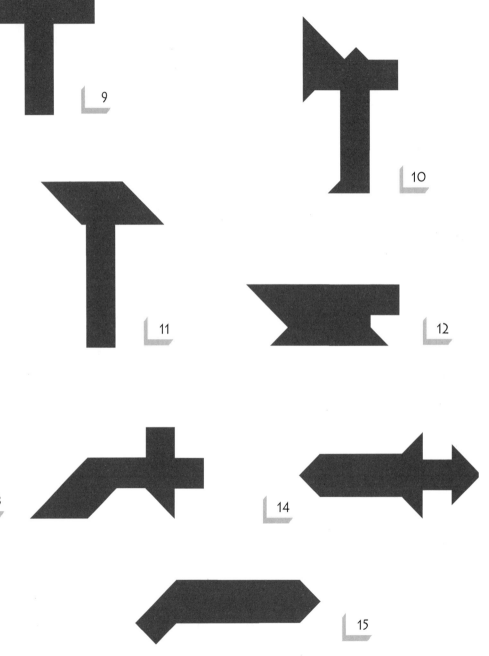

9

10

11

12

13

14

15

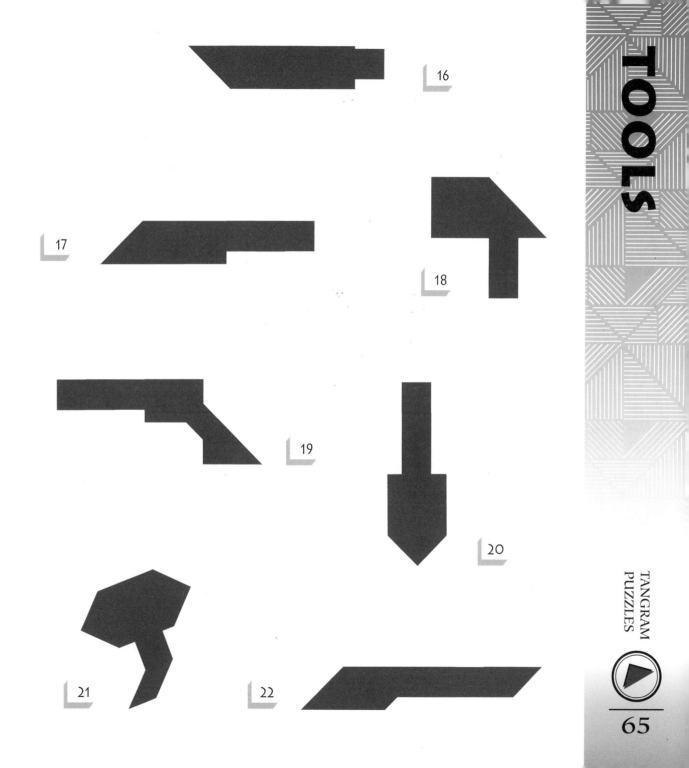

16

17

18

19

20

21

22

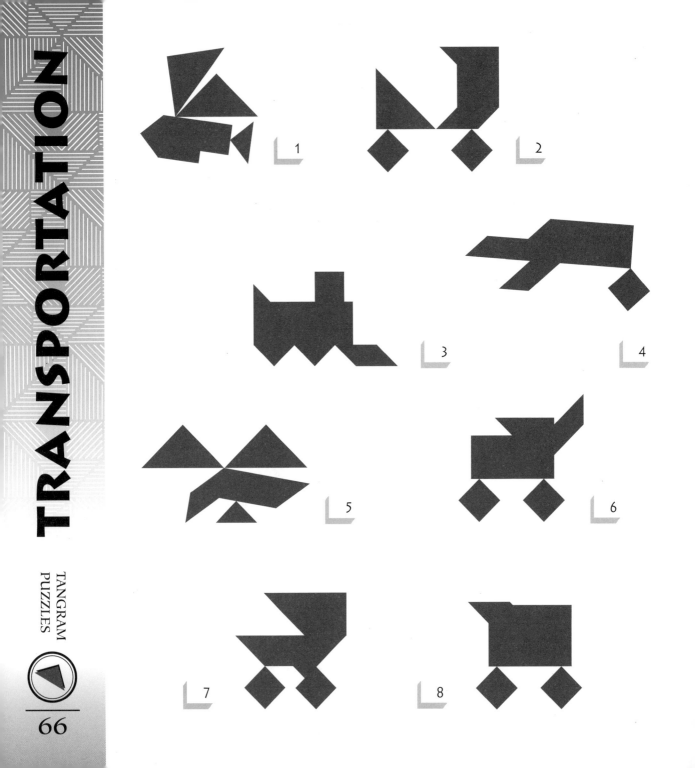

1

2

3

4

5

6

7

8

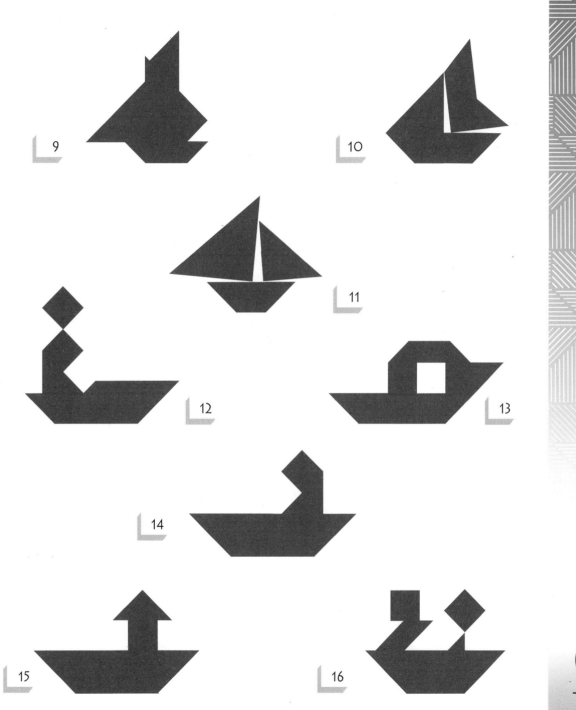

9

10

11

12

13

14

15

16

TANGRAM
PUZZLES

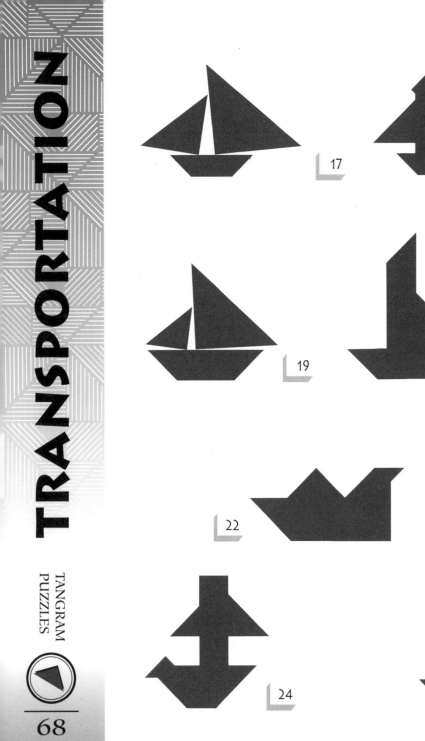

17

18

19

20

21

22

23

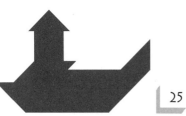

24

25

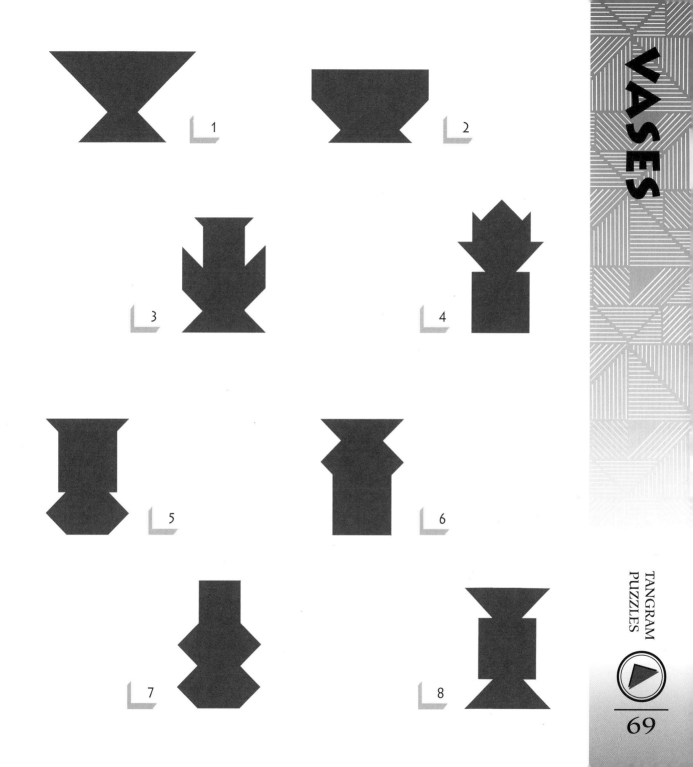

1

2

3

4

5

6

7

8

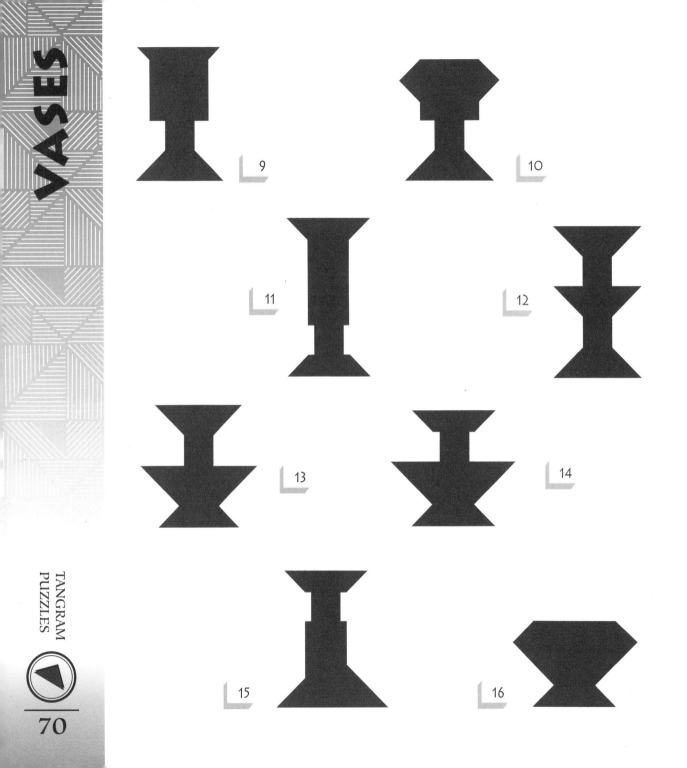

9

10

11

12

13

14

15

16

BIRDS

21 22 23 24

25 26 27 28

29 30 31 32

33 34 35 36

37 38 39 40

41 42 43

BUILDINGS

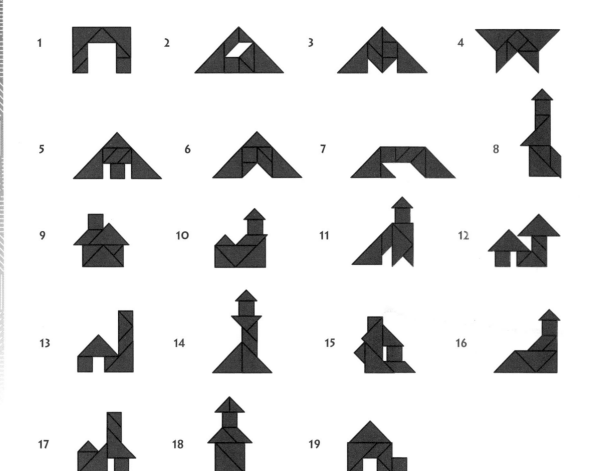

1 2 3 4

5 6 7 8

9 10 11 12

13 14 15 16

17 18 19

CATS

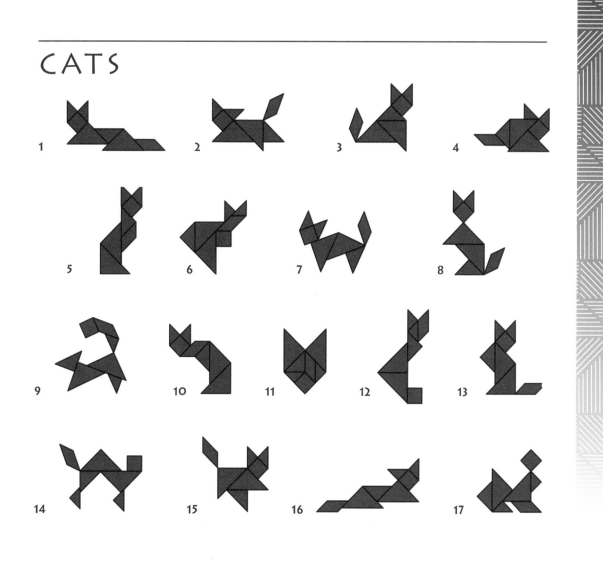

CONVEX SHAPES

 1

 2

 3

 4

 5

 6

 7

 8

9

10

 11

12

13

DOGS

 1

 2

 3

 4

 5

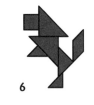 6

 7

 8

GEOMETRY

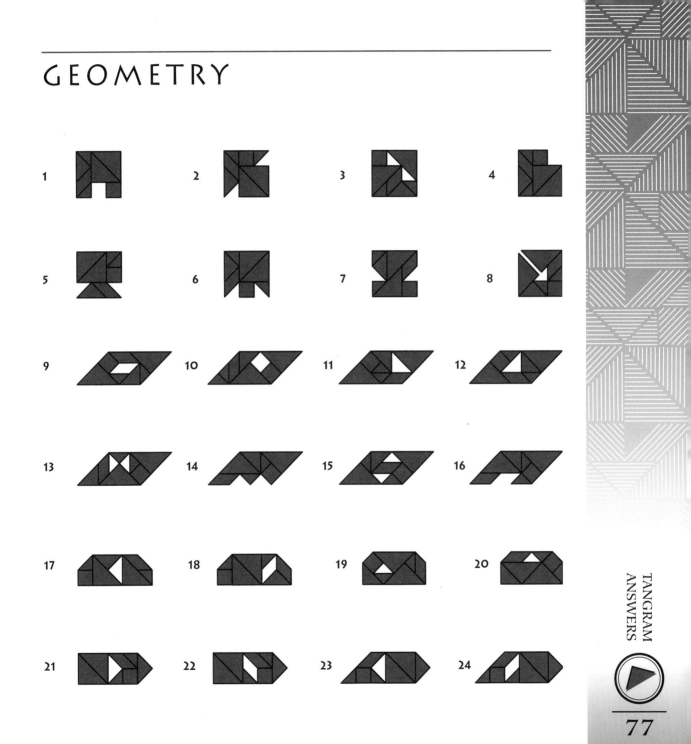

HEADS

1

2

3

4

5

6

7

8

9

10

11

12

13

14

15

16

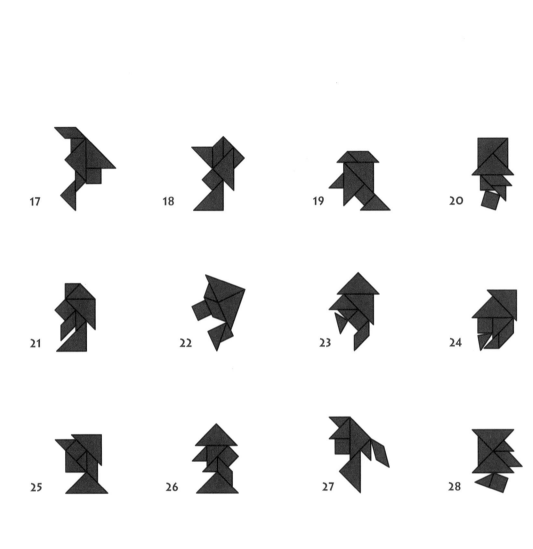

17

18

19

20

21

22

23

24

25

26

27

28

29

30

31

32

HOUSEHOLD

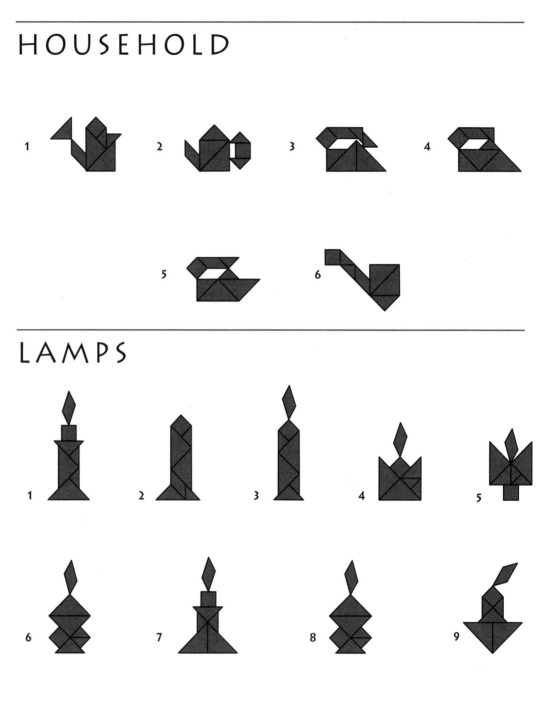

1 2 3 4

5 6

LAMPS

1 2 3 4 5

6 7 8 9

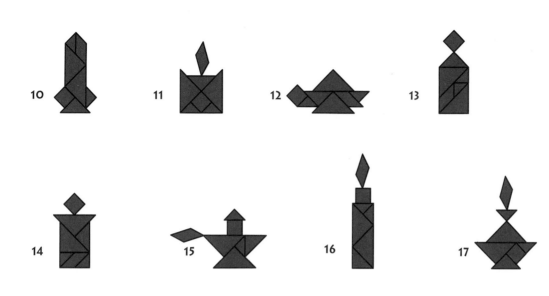

10

11

12

13

14

15

16

17

LARGE ANIMALS

1

2

3

4

5

6

7

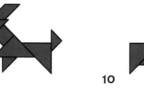

8

9

10

11

12

13

14

15

16

17

18

19

20

21

22

23

24

25

26 27 28

29 30 31

PARADOX

1 2 3 4

5 6 7 8

PARADOX

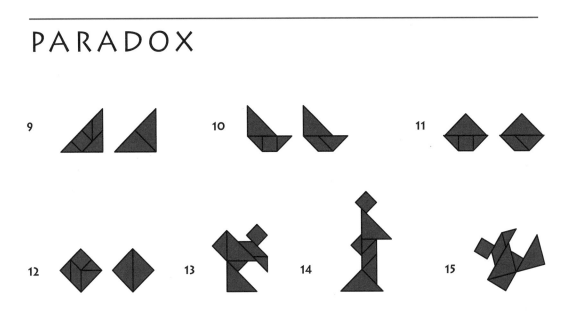

9

10

11

12

13

14

15

PEOPLE

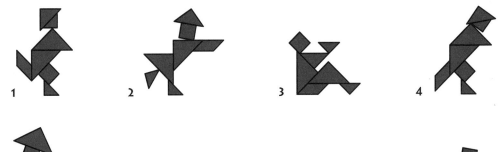

1

2

3

4

5

6

7

8

9
10
11
12
13
14
15
16
17
18
19
20
21
22
23
24
25
26
27
28

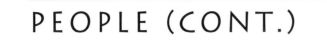

PEOPLE (CONT.)

 29

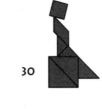 30

 31

 32

33

54

35

36

37

38

39

40

41

42

43

44

RABBITS

SEA LIFE

1

2

3

4

5

6

7

8

9

10

11

12

13

14

15

16

17

18

19

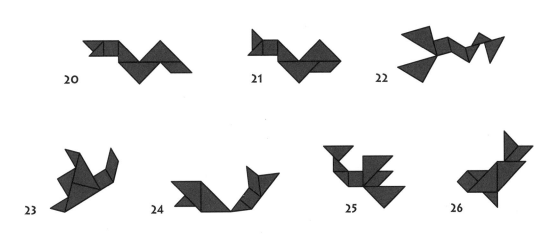

20 21 22

23 24 25 26

SHAPES

1 2 3 4

5 6 7 8 9

10 11 12 13

SHAPES (CONT.)

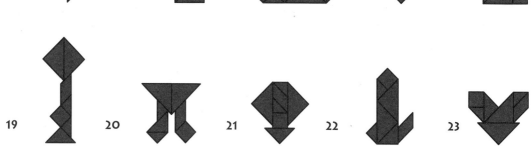

14   15   16   17   18

19   20    21   22    23

24   25   26   27   28

29   30   31   32   33

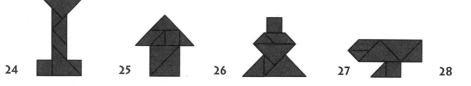

34   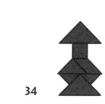 35   36    37

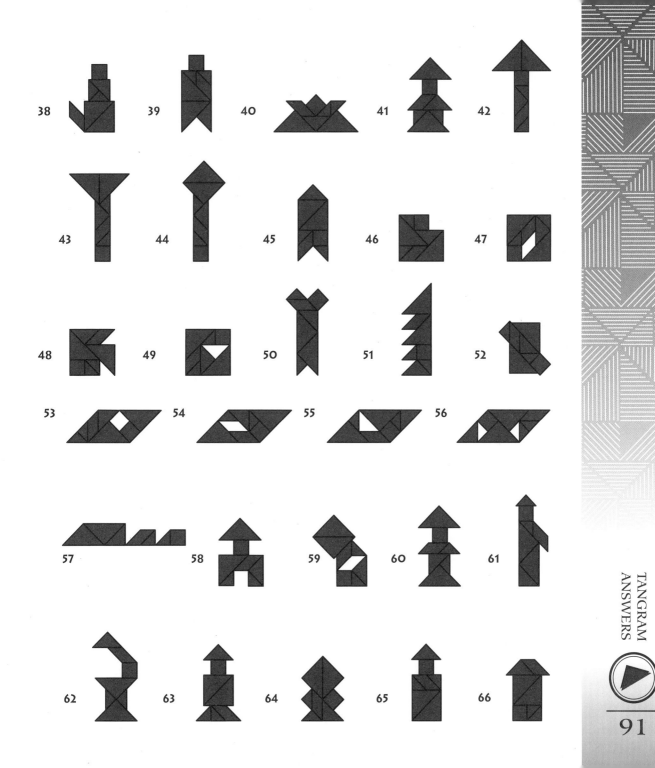

SHAPES (CONT.)

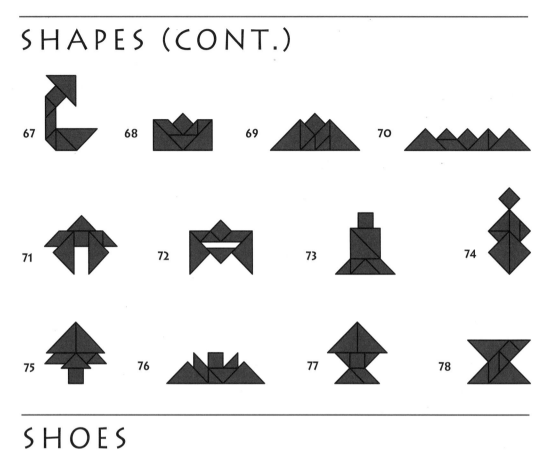

67 68 69 70

71 72 73 74

75 76 77 78

SHOES

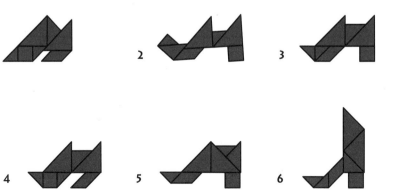

1 2 3

4 5 6 7

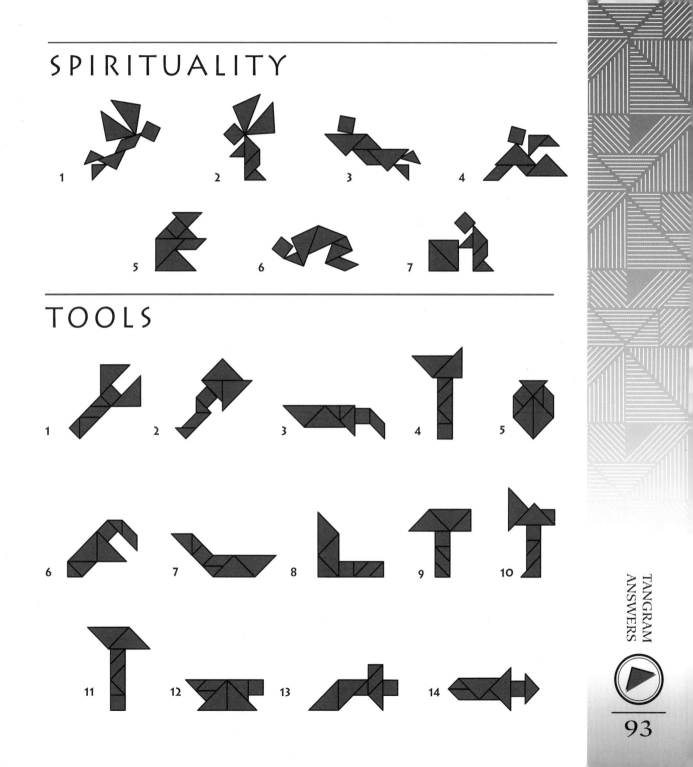

SPIRITUALITY

1   2   3   4

5   6   7

TOOLS

1   2   3   4   5

6   7   8   9   10

11   12   13   14

TOOLS (CONT.)

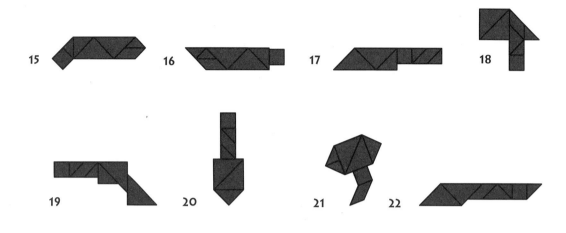

15

16

17

18

19

20

21

22

TRANSPORTATION

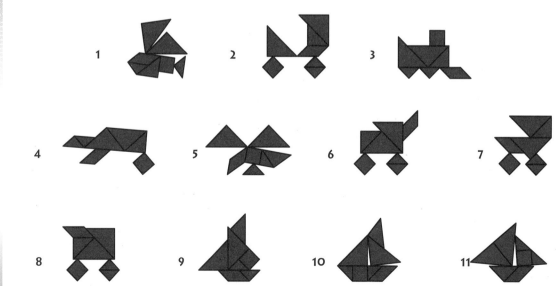

1

2

3

4

5

6

7

8

9

10

11

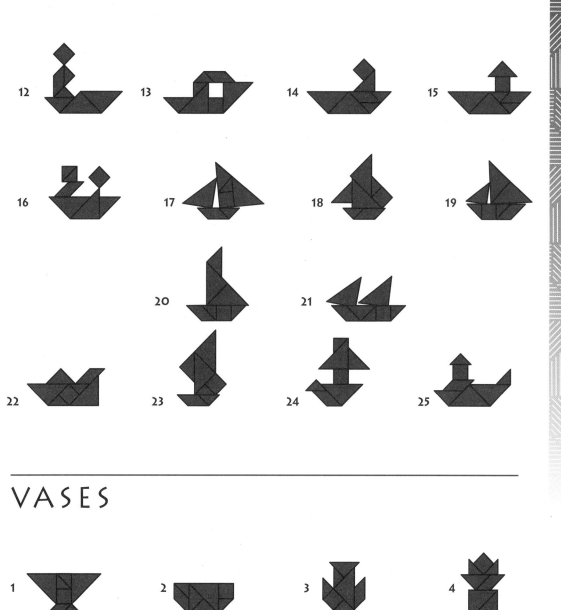

VASES

VASES (CONT.)

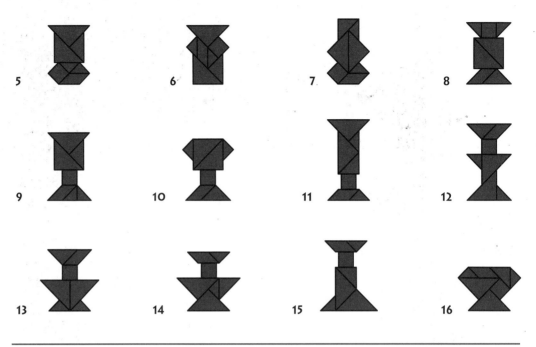

INDEX